WHAT
IN THE
WORLD
IS AN
ACRE?

AND OTHER
LAND & SEA
MEASUREMENTS

A Division of ABDO

ABDO
Publishing Company

Desirée Bussiere

Consulting Editor, Diane Craig, M.A./Reading Specialist

visit us at www.abdopublishing.com

Published by ABDO Publishing Company, a division of ABDO, P.O. Box 398166, Minneapolis, Minnesota 55439. Copyright © 2013 by Abdo Consulting Group, Inc. International copyrights reserved in all countries. No part of this book may be reproduced in any form without written permission from the publisher. SandCastle™ is a trademark and logo of ABDO Publishing Company.

Printed in the United States of America, North Mankato, Minnesota
102012
012013

 PRINTED ON RECYCLED PAPER

Editor: Liz Salzmann
Content Developer: Nancy Tuminelly
Cover and Interior Design: Colleen Dolphin, Mighty Media, Inc.
Cover and Interior Production: Kate Hartman
Photo Credits: Shutterstock

Library of Congress Cataloging-in-Publication Data

Bussierre, Desireé, 1989- author.
 What in the world is an acre? : and other land & sea measurements / Desireé Bussierre ; consulting editor, Diane Craig, M.A./reading specialist.
    pages cm. -- (Let's measure more)
Audience: 4-9
 ISBN 978-1-61783-600-8
1. Area measurement--Juvenile literature. 2. Units of measurement--Juvenile literature. I. Title.
QA465.B898 2013
530.8'1--dc23

                    2012024981

SandCastle™ Level: Transitional

SandCastle™ books are created by a team of professional educators, reading specialists, and content developers around five essential components—phonemic awareness, phonics, vocabulary, text comprehension, and fluency—to assist young readers as they develop reading skills and strategies and increase their general knowledge. All books are written, reviewed, and leveled for guided reading, early reading intervention, and Accelerated Reader® programs for use in shared, guided, and independent reading and writing activities to support a balanced approach to literacy instruction. The SandCastle™ series has four levels that correspond to early literacy development. The levels are provided to help teachers and parents select appropriate books for young readers.

Emerging Readers (no flags)　Beginning Readers (1 flag)　Transitional Readers (2 flags)　Fluent Readers (3 flags)

Contents

Earth's surface is made of land and water. People measure land and water in different ways.

measure on land & sea?

Chains are used to measure **distance** on land. There are 80 chains in one mile.

In the United States, chains are used mostly in farming.

a chain?

Kate lives on a farm. They use chains to measure the fields.

Acres are used to measure land area. A football field is about 1 acre.

an acre?

Nick's family has 20 acres of land in the country. They go there for vacation. Nick likes to ride his bike there.

A survey township is a **unit** of land. It is 6 miles on each side.

It is used mostly for land that no one lives on.

survey township?

Stacy's dad is a **surveyor**. He works for the government. He measures survey townships. He marks them on a map.

A section is part of a survey township. A survey township has 36 sections. Land is sold in sections.

section?

Leo's parents bought a section of land. They built a cabin on it.

A Hectare is a **metric** measurement. It is used to measure land area. One hectare equals 10,000 square meters. That's about 12,000 square yards.

a hectare?

Joy is visiting New York City. She loves the Statue of Liberty. Its base covers about one hectare of land.

Nautical miles are used to measure **distance** on water.

One nautical mile equals 6,076 feet (1,852 m).

nautical mile?

Eric's family goes deep sea fishing. They are 6 **nautical** miles from shore. Eric catches a big fish!

Knots are used to measure the speed of ships. Knots are the number of **nautical** miles a ship goes in one hour. One knot equals about 1.15 miles per hour (1.85 kph).

a knot?

Rita is on a **cruise** with her family. The ship goes 20 knots.

Fathoms are used to measure how deep water is. One fathom equals 6 feet (1.8 m).

a fathom?

Jim swims in the lake. The water is 2 fathoms deep.

Fun facts

⇨ Edmund invented the chain in 1620.

⇨ The acre was based on how much land an ox could **plow** in one day.

⇨ Survey townships are only used in the United States.

⇨ Knots used to be measured with a rope. The rope had knots tied in it.

Quiz

Read each sentence below. Then decide whether it is true or false.

1. There are 80 chains in a mile. True or False?

2. A basketball court is about one acre. True or False?

3. There are 36 sections in a township. True or False?

4. Knots are used to measure the speed of cars. True or False?

5. One fathom equals 6 feet. True or False?

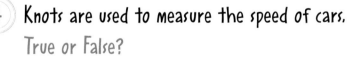

Answers: 1. True 2. False 3. True 4. False 5. True

Glossary

cruise — a vacation on a ship.

distance — the amount of space between two places.

metric — related to the measurement system based on the meter and kilogram.

nautical — related to sailors, navigation, or ships.

plow — to cut, lift, and turn over soil.

surveyor — someone whose job is to measure land for maps.

unit — an amount used as a standard of measurement.